D0535930

C.1

Major US Historical Wars

THE AMERICAN REVOLUTION

John Ziff

Mason Crest
Philadelphia

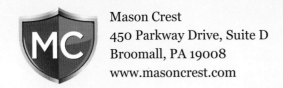

Mason Crest
450 Parkway Drive, Suite D
Broomall, PA 19008
www.masoncrest.com

© 2016 by Mason Crest, an imprint of National Highlights, Inc.
All rights reserved. No part of this publication may be reproduced or transmitted in any form or by any means, electronic or mechanical, including photocopying, recording, taping, or any information storage and retrieval system, without permission from the publisher.

Printed and bound in the United States of America.
CPSIA Compliance Information: Batch #MUW2015.
For further information, contact Mason Crest at 1-866-MCP-Book.

3 5 7 9 8 6 4 2
Library of Congress Cataloging-in-Publication Data

ISBN: 978-1-4222-3353-5 (hc)
ISBN: 978-1-4222-8593-0 (ebook)

Major US Historical Wars series ISBN: 978-1-4222-3352-8

Picture Credits: Architect of the Capitol: 19, 29, 38, 55; collection of the Fort Ticonderoga Museum: 26; the Nathanael Greene Homestead: 51; Google Art Project: 28; Independence National Historical Park: 40, 41; Library of Congress: 1, 10, 11, 17, 33, 35, 36, 46, 47; from The Story of the Revolution by Henry Cabot Lodge: 49; National Archives: 13, 43, 56; National Guard Heritage Series: 7, 21, 25, 31; Daniel M. Silva / Shutterstock: 44; from the collection of the State of South Carolina: 52; US Senate Collection: 23, 42.

About the Author: John Ziff is a writer and editor who lives near Philadelphia.

TABLE OF CONTENTS

KEY ICONS TO LOOK FOR:

Text-dependent questions: These questions send the reader back to the text for more careful attention to the evidence presented there.

Words to understand: These words with their easy-to-understand definitions will increase the reader's understanding of the text, while building vocabulary skills.

Series glossary of key terms: This back-of-the book glossary contains terminology used throughout this series. Words found here increase the reader's ability to read and comprehend higher-level books and articles in this field.

Research projects: Readers are pointed toward areas of further inquiry connected to each chapter. Suggestions are provided for projects that encourage deeper research and analysis.

Sidebars: This boxed material within the main text allows readers to build knowledge, gain insights, explore possibilities, and broaden their perspectives by weaving together additional information to provide realistic and holistic perspectives.

Other Titles in This Series

Introduction

by Series Consultant
Jason Musteen

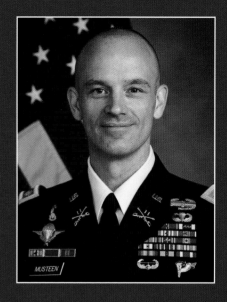

Lt. Col. Jason R. Musteen is a U.S. Army Cavalry officer and combat veteran who has held various command and staff jobs in Infantry and Cavalry units. He holds a PhD in Napoleonic History from Florida State University and currently serves as Chief of the Division of Military History at the U.S. Military Academy at West Point. He has appeared frequently on the History Channel.

Why should middle and high school students read about and study American wars? Does doing so promote militarism or instill misguided patriotism? The United States of America was born at war, and the nation has spent the majority of its existence at war. Our wars have demonstrated both the best and worst of who we are. They have freed millions from oppression and slavery, but they have also been a vehicle for fear, racism, and imperialism. Warfare has shaped the geography of our nation, informed our laws, and it even inspired our national anthem. It has united us and it has divided us.

Valley Forge, the *USS Constitution*, Gettysburg, Wounded Knee, Belleau Wood, Normandy, Midway, Inchon, the A Shau Valley, and Fallujah are all a part of who we are as a nation. Therefore, the study of America at war does not necessarily make students or educators militaristic; rather, it makes them thorough and responsible. To ignore warfare, which has been such a significant part of our history, would not only leave our education incomplete, it would also be negligent.

For those who wish to avoid warfare, or to at least limit its horrors, understanding conflict is a worthwhile, and even necessary, pursuit. The American author John Steinbeck once said, "all war is a symptom of man's failure as a thinking animal." If Steinbeck is right, then we must think.

And we must think about war. We must study war with all its attendant horrors and miseries. We must study the heroes and the villains. We must study the root causes of our wars, how we chose to fight them, and what has been achieved or lost through them. The study of America at war is an essential component of being an educated American.

Still, there is something compelling in our military history that makes the study not only necessary, but enjoyable, as well. The desperation that drove Washington's soldiers across the Delaware River at the end of 1776 intensifies an exciting story of American success against all odds. The sailors and Marines who planted the American flag on the rocky peak of Mount Suribachi on Iwo Jima still speak to us of courage and sacrifice. The commitment that led American airmen to the relief of West Berlin in the Cold War inspires us to the service of others. The stories of these men and women are exciting, and they matter. We should study them. Moreover, for all the suffering it brings, war has at times served noble purposes for the United States. Americans can find common pride in the chronicle of the Continental Army's few victories and many defeats in the struggle for independence. We can accept that despite inflicting deep national wounds and lingering division, our Civil War yielded admirable results in the abolition of slavery and eventual national unity. We can celebrate American resolve and character as the nation rallied behind a common cause to free the world from tyranny in World War II. We can do all that without necessarily promoting war.

In this series of books, Mason Crest Publishers offers students a foundation for the study of American wars. Building on the expertise of a team of accomplished authors, the series explores the causes, conduct, and consequences of America's wars. It also presents educators with the means to take their students to a deeper understanding of the material through additional research and project ideas. I commend it to all students and to those who educate them to become responsible, informed Americans.

Chapter 1:

SEEDS OF REVOLUTION

As dawn broke on May 28, 1754, the French soldiers camped in the hollow began to stir. They stretched their legs. They gathered dry twigs for cooking fires. In the dim light, they failed to notice shadowy figures creeping onto the rock ledges that overlooked the hollow.

Presently, one of the French soldiers heard a noise or saw movement

(Above) American militiamen attack a band of Native Americans in western Virginia during the French and Indian War (1754–1763). This conflict, pitting the French and their Native American allies against the British Army and colonists in North America, soon expanded into a world war, known in Europe as the Seven Years' War.

WORDS TO UNDERSTAND IN THIS CHAPTER

boycott—to refuse to buy a product as a means of protest.

delegate—a representative to a convention or conference.

detachment—a group of soldiers separated from a larger military force for a particular mission.

duty—a tax on imported goods.

liberty—the freedom to live as one chooses, without undue interference from government; the ability to enjoy economic, political, and social rights.

militia—a group of civilians who train for military service and may be called to serve in an emergency.

musket—a heavy, shoulder-fired gun that was the standard firearm for infantry soldiers in the Revolutionary War.

Parliament—the legislature of Great Britain, consisting of the House of Lords and the House of Commons.

Patriot—a colonist who supported independence from Great Britain in the Revolutionary War era.

petition—a formal request to a government official or person in authority.

redcoat—a soldier in the British army.

revenue—money collected by a government (for example, through taxes).

above. He shouted a warning to his comrades. They scrambled for their weapons as musket fire erupted from the rim of the hollow. After a fight lasting no more than 15 minutes, the surrounded French surrendered. A dozen were dead or dying. About 20 survivors were taken prisoner.

The attackers turned out to be a ***detachment*** of Virginia ***militia***. Their commander was an eager but inexperienced 22-year-old named George Washington.

The French and Indian War

The deadly skirmish took place at a remote spot dubbed Jumonville Glen, about 40 miles south of present-day Pittsburgh. The clash came about because of a simmering dispute over the "Ohio Country." That region lay to the west of the British colonies of Virginia, Maryland, and Pennsylvania. Great Britain claimed the Ohio Country, and colonists from Virginia were determined to settle it.

But there was a problem. France also claimed the Ohio Country. According to the French, the region was part of New France, a vast colonial territory that covered much of the interior of North America. New France extended from Canada in the north to the Gulf of Mexico in the south.

The encounter at Jumonville Glen involved fewer than 100 men in all. But it ignited a major conflict. British colonists called it the French and Indian War. Many thousands of British regular soldiers were sent to North America, as Great Britain moved to eliminate the French threat to its 13 mainland colonies. France responded in kind. Colonial militias fought alongside the regiments of regular soldiers. Each side also had Indian allies.

By 1756, the fighting in North America pushed Great Britain and France to declare war on each other directly. The Seven Years' War, as the expanded conflict came to be called, had far-flung battlefields in Europe, South America, Asia, and Africa.

British forces eventually triumphed. The war officially ended with the signing of the Treaty of Paris on February 10, 1763. By the terms of the treaty, France gave up its claims to all territory in North America east of the Mississippi River. That vast area was now recognized as belonging to the king of Great Britain. France also ceded Canada to Great Britain.

By all appearances, Great Britain had secured a tremendous victory. Its overseas empire had greatly expanded. With the French threat eliminated, the 13 North American colonies seemed on the cusp of a new era of growth and prosperity. In fact, Britain's victory contained the seeds of conflict with the very colonies it had just successfully defended.

A Controversial Proclamation

The Seven Years' War had cost Great Britain a huge sum of money. By war's end, the Crown was deeply in debt. As they grappled with how to handle the debt, King George III and his ministers made a series of decisions regarding the future of the North American colonies.

In October 1763, King George issued a proclamation. It dealt with several important issues. But for people in the 13 colonies, one issue in particular stood out. The Royal Proclamation of 1763 barred colonists from settling west of the Appalachians, a mountain system running from Canada through northern Georgia. Those who had already moved across the Appalachians were ordered to move back. The land was to be reserved for Indians. This, the king and his ministers believed, would avoid constant—and expensive—warfare between colonists and Indians.

The proclamation upset many colonists. They coveted new land. In the end, colonists simply ignored the proclamation's ban on settling west of the Appalachians. Clearly, Great Britain couldn't count on the American colonists' blind obedience to royal authority.

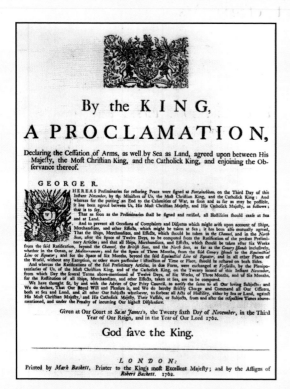

A proclamation issued by King George III announcing the end of the French and Indian War. After the conflict ended, the British government imposed new taxes on the colonies, and prevented Americans from settling in lands to the west of the Appalachian Mountains. These actions made many Americans angry and resentful.

Raising Revenue

In 1764, Parliament—Great Britain's legislature—passed the American *Revenue* Act. Popularly known as the Sugar Act, the law imposed a *duty* (tax) of three pence per gallon on all molasses imported into the American colonies.

Colonists didn't like the Sugar Act. Molasses, which is derived from sugarcane, was used to make rum. The import duty hurt the colonial rum industry. Still, most colonists saw the Sugar Act as a measure to regulate trade. That was something colonists believed Great Britain had every right to do. And anyway, most colonists weren't directly affected by the import duty on molasses, or by the Sugar Act's other provisions.

The same couldn't be said of the Stamp Act, passed by Parliament in March 1765 and slated to go into effect on November 1 of that year. It applied to common legal documents almost every colonist would need at some time, such as marriage licenses, wills, deeds, and contracts. It applied to newspapers, almanacs, and pamphlets. It even applied to playing cards. The Stamp Act required that all these items be on paper bearing a royal revenue stamp.

The cost would vary according to the type of printed material in question. But all money raised would be used to offset the Crown's expenses for the defense of the colonies. Still, the Stamp Act met with furious opposition from colonists. Why?

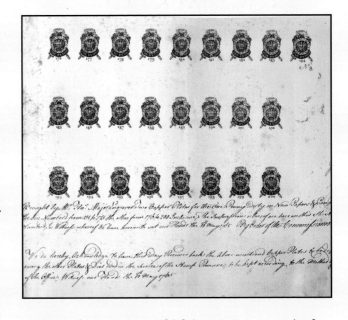

A sheet of tax stamps, which in 1765 were required on all legal documents, permits, contracts, newspapers, pamphlets, and playing cards in the American colonies. The money raised from the Stamp Act tax was to be used to help pay the cost of protecting the colonies.

A Question of Representation

The 13 colonies had developed separately, and their colonial governments differed in certain details. The basic structure, though, consisted of a governor, a governor's council, and an assembly.

In most colonies, the governor was appointed directly by the Crown. Governors, in turn, usually appointed members of the council. Councils advised the governor and performed various other functions. They tended to be closely allied with the governor.

In all 13 colonies, voters elected representatives to the colonial assembly (though the right to vote was generally limited to white men age 21 or over who owned a certain amount of property). The assembly had sole authority to levy taxes in the colony. This reflected an idea of enormous importance in the development of English government. A ruler, it was held, didn't have the right simply to impose taxes on his subjects. The people had to grant him permission to tax. And the way they did so was through their elected representatives.

In Great Britain, it was firmly established that no new taxes could be levied without parliamentary approval. Members of the House of Commons, the lower chamber of Parliament, were elected. Parliamentary approval of taxation was viewed as a cornerstone of English *liberty*. If a king had unchecked power to tax, he could easily deprive his subjects of their property.

Great Britain had never attempted to impose a direct tax on the 13 colonies. Yet that's clearly what the Stamp Act was. The act had been passed by Parliament rather than dictated by the king. But colonists

Some British officials argued that the American colonies enjoyed *virtual representation* in Parliament. According to this idea, every member of Parliament represented every British subject in the empire, not just the people from the member's district.

didn't think that mattered, because they didn't get to vote for members of Parliament. The British government was seeking to tax them without their consent. Their rights as British subjects, they believed, were being violated.

Backlash

In May 1765, shortly after news of the Stamp Act's passage reached the colonies, Virginia's House of Burgesses took action. The elected assembly passed a series of resolutions. The Virginia Resolves, as they came to be called, laid out reasons the Stamp Act taxes were illegal and invalid.

Colonial newspapers widely reprinted the Virginia Resolves. The assemblies of other colonies also drafted resolutions detailing their opposition to the Stamp Act. They *petitioned* the British government to repeal the law.

Some colonists weren't content with legislative resolutions or petitions to London. They favored more persuasive tactics. Secretive groups calling themselves the Sons of Liberty formed. In New York City, the Sons of Liberty posted threatening notices on street corners and on the doors of public buildings. "The first Man that either distributes or makes use of Stampt Paper," the notices warned, "let him take Care of his House, Person, and Effects." The notices were signed *Vox Populi*—Latin for "Voice of the People."

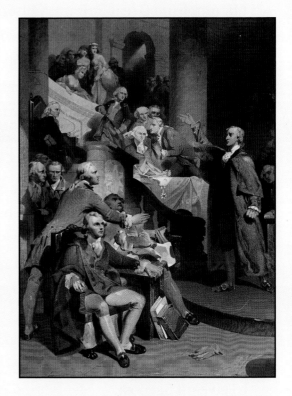

Patrick Henry presents resolutions against the Stamp Act to the Virginia House of Burgesses, May 30, 1765. The resolutions asserted that the colonists could not be taxed because they were not represented in Parliament.

In several cities, mobs prevented the distribution of stamped paper. Rioters also destroyed the homes and offices of royally appointed stamp commissioners.

Glimmers of Unity

In June, the Massachusetts assembly had sent a letter to the assemblies of the other colonies. It called for a meeting to discuss the Stamp Act. Nine of the 13 colonies sent representatives to the meeting. Called the Stamp Act Congress, it convened in New York City in early October.

The mere fact that the Stamp Act Congress took place was significant. The colonies weren't accustomed to working together. As yet, colonists had no sense of belonging to an American nation that was distinct from Great Britain. Colonists considered themselves British subjects first and foremost. Beyond that, they tended to identify strongly with their particular colony. So, for example, Virginians were unlikely to recognize that they had much in common with New Yorkers or Rhode Islanders.

But *delegates* to the Stamp Act Congress put aside their differences. After nearly two weeks of discussion and debate, they approved a document known as the Declaration of Rights. It expressed the colonists' "sincere devotion" to King George but systematically laid out their case against the Stamp Act. Petitions were drafted asking Parliament and the king to repeal the act. The Stamp Act Congress finished its work on October 25.

One week later, the Stamp Act went into effect. But not a single penny was collected from the stamp tax anywhere in the colonies. Threats and mob violence had convinced every stamp commissioner to give up his post.

Weeks passed, then months. The impasse continued. Finally, on March 18, 1766, Parliament voted to repeal the Stamp Act. In the colonies, news of the repeal was greeted with jubilation. There would be no taxation without representation. The principle that the colonists possessed the same rights as people born in England had been vindicated. Or so it seemed.

Few colonists either heard about, or recognized the significance of, an act Parliament passed on the same day it repealed the Stamp Act. The Declaratory Act stated that the king and Parliament had "full power and authority to make laws and statutes . . . to bind the colonies and people of *America* . . . in all cases whatsoever."

The Townshend Acts

In June 1767, Parliament passed a series of measures devised by Charles Townshend. He was Britain's top minister for financial matters.

The centerpiece of the so-called Townshend Acts was the Revenue Act of 1767. It imposed new import duties on glass, lead, paint, paper, and tea brought into the colonies.

Another law, the Commissioners of Customs Act, was designed to put teeth into British efforts to collect the Townshend duties. It created a customs board for the American colonies. Headquartered in Boston, the board had sweeping authority to enforce customs regulations.

The Vice-Admiralty Court Act was neither conceived by Charles Townshend nor passed by Parliament. Yet it became an important tool for upholding the Townshend duties. Put forward by British Treasury officials and approved by King George in July 1768, the law set up special courts to try colonists accused of smuggling or other customs violations. In these courts, there were no jury trials. Judges appointed by the Crown decided all cases. And the judges received cash bonuses each time they found a defendant guilty.

Townshend didn't anticipate much colonial opposition to his program. Like other British officials, he believed the Stamp Act had riled colonists so much because it would have imposed a tax inside the colonies. The new taxes, by contrast, were in the form of import duties.

But for colonists, it didn't matter how a tax was structured. In their view, no tax was legal unless approved by their own representatives. Other provisions of the new laws also inflamed the colonists. The vice-admiralty courts were especially troubling. Like taxation without representation, the courts violated a basic right guaranteed by England's constitution: the right of citizens accused of a crime to a trial by jury.

Rising Tensions

In February 1768, the Massachusetts assembly approved a letter to be sent to other colonial assemblies. The "circular letter" laid out objections to the Townshend Acts. It suggested that the colonial legislatures consider unified action.

That suggestion made British officials nervous. The Massachusetts assembly was ordered to retract its circular letter. The assembly refused. The governor of Massachusetts promptly dissolved the assembly.

Tensions simmered. In June, a British warship sent to Boston seized the merchant vessel *Liberty* on suspicion of smuggling. The *Liberty* was owned by one of the Massachusetts colony's most prominent citizens, John Hancock. Its seizure sparked a massive riot on Boston's waterfront.

Britain's secretary of state for the colonies, Lord Hillsborough, responded to the unrest by dispatching several thousand British soldiers to Boston. The **redcoats** began arriving on October 1, 1768.

Throughout the 13 colonies, some people refused to buy British products as a way to protest the Townshend Acts. Merchants in port cities such as Boston, Philadelphia, and Charleston signed non-importation agreements. They pledged to stop ordering goods from Great Britain.

As a result of the **boycotts**, British trade with the colonies plummeted. British manufacturers and merchants felt the pinch. Some grumbled that Parliament should reconsider its policies. By early 1770, Great Britain had a new prime minister, Frederick North, who agreed. Lord North convinced Parliament to repeal all the Townshend duties except the one on tea. That was kept to uphold the principle that Great Britain had the *right* to tax the colonies.

The Boston Massacre

Meanwhile, some Bostonians seethed at the continuing presence of redcoats in their midst. To them, the British soldiers seemed like an occupying army.

Resentments boiled over on the cold evening of March 5, 1770. A crowd of rowdy colonists milled around the Boston Customs House, jeering at a British soldier posted to guard the building. They pelted the soldier with snowballs and stones. When a squad of reinforcements arrived, the angry crowd pressed closer. A club hurled from the crowd knocked down one of

Paul Revere's engraving of the March 1770 clash between Patriots and Redcoats became the most famous picture of the Boston Massacre. According to Revere's version, British troops opened fire on defenseless civilians. This was not quite accurate, but was useful as propaganda to stir up colonial support for the Patriots.

the soldiers. His *musket* discharged, perhaps accidentally. In the confusion, the other redcoats fired into the crowd. Five colonists died as a result.

People throughout the 13 colonies were shocked when they learned about what came to be called the Boston Massacre. Still, the incident didn't trigger widespread unrest. In fact, a period of relative calm in the colonies soon followed. News that *Parliament* had repealed most of the Townshend duties reassured many colonists. The British, it appeared, weren't set on trampling colonial rights.

Some colonial leaders, however, remained suspicious of British intentions. In 1772, two Massachusetts leaders—Samuel Adams and Dr. Joseph Warren—helped establish a "committee of correspondence" in Boston. Its purpose was to inform colonists elsewhere of developments and to encourage coordinated action against objectionable British policies. Soon, a host of committees of correspondence had sprung up throughout the 13 colonies. They formed a network by which *Patriots*—people determined to defend colonial rights—communicated with one another.

The Tea Party and the Coercive Acts

In May 1773, Parliament passed the Tea Act. The new law would have the effect of making tea cheaper in the colonies. Parliament believed this would induce colonists to start buying British tea again. And by paying the Townshend duties on that tea, colonists would be conceding that Parliament had the right to tax them.

Patriots had other ideas, however. Hostile crowds in Philadelphia and New York prevented ships carrying tea from being unloaded. The ships' captains were eventually persuaded to take their cargo to England. In Boston, the Sons of Liberty also blocked tea from being brought ashore. But the tea ships remained in the harbor.

On the night of December 16, 1773, Patriots—some of them dressed as Indians—rowed out to three tea ships at anchor in Boston Harbor. They proceeded to dump more than 45 tons of tea into the water.

Bostonians dressed as Indians throw crates of tea into Boston Harbor, December 16, 1773. In response to the Boston Tea Party, the British government closed the port and imposed strict rules on the Massachusetts colony.

The Boston Tea Party, as the incident came to be called, infuriated British officials. In 1774, Parliament passed four laws known collectively as the Coercive Acts. Three of the acts were intended to bring the defiant Massachusetts colonists to heel. The Boston Port Act closed Boston to all shipping until Massachusetts paid for the tea that had been destroyed. The Massachusetts Government Act gave the royal governor authority to appoint officials who had previously been elected. It also banned town meetings. The Administration of Government Act allowed the royal governor to move trials of Massachusetts officials to England, where verdicts the Crown wanted were more likely. Under the Quartering Act, any colony could be required to house British troops in inns, barns, or unused buildings.

The harshness of Parliament's actions stunned Massachusetts citizens. Patriot leaders convinced most of the colony's counties to shut down their courts rather than comply with the new laws. In Suffolk County—which included Boston—Patriots issued a bold declaration called the Suffolk Resolves. It denied that Massachusetts was under any obligation to obey the Coercive Acts. It urged the withholding of tax payments to the colonial government. And, most radically, it proposed the establishment of a "provincial Congress." The Resolves said the provincial Congress would function as the lawful government of Massachusetts until the Coercive Acts were repealed.

Patriots in the other colonies also hated the Coercive Acts. Many referred to them as the Intolerable Acts. But what could be done about the laws? Committees of correspondence called for a meeting to discuss options. Twelve of the 13 colonies—Georgia was the exception—sent delegates to Philadelphia for the First Continental Congress. It met from September 5 to October 26, 1774. The delegates approved the Suffolk Resolves, signaling that the other colonies would stand by Massachusetts. The delegates agreed to cease all trade with Great Britain unless the Coercive Acts were repealed by December. They also agreed to convene again in May 1775.

"The Die Is Now Cast"

Most Patriots still believed their differences with Great Britain could be resolved. They probably wouldn't have felt that way had they known of a September 1774 letter written by King George III. "The die is now cast," the king informed his prime minister, Lord North. "The colonies must either submit or triumph."

 TEXT-DEPENDENT QUESTIONS

1. Why was the British government in debt in 1763?
2. What would the Stamp Act do? Why did the act anger colonists?
3. What event spurred Parliament to pass the Coercive Acts?

 RESEARCH PROJECT

Read about one of the 13 colonies. Write a one-page report summarizing the colony's history, from its founding to 1774.

Chapter 2:

A GLORIOUS CAUSE

During the first months of 1775, the situation in Massachusetts grew ever more tense. The Massachusetts Provincial Congress met regularly in the town of Concord, about 17 miles west of Boston. It claimed to be the lawful government of the colony. Special patriot militia companies trained hard. They seemed to be preparing for a showdown with the British. They called themselves Minutemen. They said they could be ready for action at a minute's notice.

(Above) Colonial minutemen fire on British troops at the North Bridge near Concord, Massachusetts, in April 1775. Fighting at Lexington and Concord marked the start of the

WORDS TO UNDERSTAND IN THIS CHAPTER

breastworks—chest-high defensive works, usually constructed quickly by digging a trench and piling the soil in front of it.

casualties—in warfare, the toll of soldiers who are killed, wounded, captured, or missing after a battle.

Hessians—German professional soldiers hired by the British.

Loyalist—a colonist who supported Great Britain during the American Revolution.

redoubt—a strong, usually temporary fortification.

The Revolution Begins

Blood was finally spilled on April 19. Seven hundred redcoats had been dispatched from Boston the previous night. Their mission was to seize gunpowder and other military supplies the Patriots were believed to have stockpiled in Concord. If possible, they were also to capture Patriot leaders Samuel Adams and John Hancock.

The British mission was supposed to be secret. But Patriots found out about it. Militias were alerted.

Shortly after sunrise, redcoats clashed with a small group of militiamen at the village of Lexington. Later, when the British reached Concord, Minutemen from surrounding areas began converging on the town. Colonists routed a British detachment guarding Concord's North Bridge.

The British began a retreat. But swarms of militia ambushed them and conducted relentless hit-and-run attacks. The colonists kept up the fight even after a thousand-man relief column met the retreating redcoats at Lexington.

Around dusk, the exhausted British finally reached safety just north of Boston. The British had suffered more than 70 dead and about 175 wounded in the day's fighting. About 50 colonists had been killed and about 40 wounded. The Revolutionary War had begun.

The city of Boston sat at the end of the Shawmut Peninsula. A narrow neck connected it to the mainland. Relatively small numbers of soldiers could easily block the neck. And by April 20, some 15,000 colonial militiamen had arrived at the shoreline around the peninsula. Many were from Massachusetts. But many others had marched from the other New England colonies, Rhode Island, Connecticut, and New Hampshire. The militias had Boston's redcoat regiments hemmed in.

An Army and a Commander

On May 10, the Second Continental Congress convened in Philadelphia. As had been the case the year before, all the colonies except Georgia were represented. Georgia finally sent a delegation in July.

A month earlier, on June 14, Congress had voted to create an army for the colonies. At first, the Continental Army would consist solely of the New England militias besieging Boston. But additional units would be raised from all the colonies.

To lead the Continental Army, Congress chose George Washington. During the French and Indian War, he'd served as a colonel in Virginia's militia regiment. That made him as qualified for command as just about

George Washington was a respected Virginia planter who had commanded American soldiers during the French and Indian War. In June 1775 the Continental Congress chose Washington to lead an American army that was formed in Massachusetts.

anyone in the colonies. Still, Washington couldn't come close to matching the senior British commanders he'd be facing in military training or experience. And he knew this. All he could do, he told Congress, was to "exert every power I possess in . . . support of the glorious cause."

The Bloody Battle of Bunker Hill

On June 17, before Washington had set out from Philadelphia to assume command of the army, a major battle was fought near Boston. The previous night, Patriot militias had dug trenches and erected earthen fortifications on the Charlestown Peninsula. The peninsula lay north of Boston, across the Charles River. Its southern tip was just a quarter mile from northern Boston.

The Patriots had fortified two hills on the Charlestown Peninsula. Breed's Hill, the closer of the two to Boston, was about 60 feet high. Behind it, Bunker Hill rose 110 feet. If the Patriots placed cannons on the high ground, they might be able to threaten British positions in Boston.

British warships pounded the Patriot fortifications from the surrounding waters. But the shelling had little effect. Troops would be needed to dislodge the rebels.

Four thousand redcoats had recently arrived in Boston by ship. That brought the total number of British troops in the city to more than 8,000. In addition, three top British generals—William Howe, Henry Clinton, and John Burgoyne—had been sent from England. They were to assist General Thomas Gage. He was the royal governor of Massachusetts as well as commander-in-chief of British forces in North America.

Dr. Joseph Warren, president of the Massachusetts Provincial Assembly, was killed at the Battle of Bunker Hill. Though he held a commission as a major general in the Massachusetts militia, Warren had chosen to fight as an ordinary private.

General Gage and the three other generals discussed how to deal with the situation on Charlestown Peninsula. Clinton wanted to land troops behind the Patriot positions, at the narrow Charlestown Neck. Gage, Howe, and Burgoyne rejected that idea in favor of a frontal assault. They had a low opinion of the Americans' fighting abilities.

By early afternoon on July 17, more than 2,000 redcoats had been landed on the southern shore of Charlestown Peninsula. About 1,500 colonial militiamen awaited their attack. The militiamen occupied the **redoubt** on Breed's Hill and a line of **breastworks** and rail fencing on the left flank. This line extended down the slope of the hill to the Mystic River.

Around 3 pm, the redcoats advanced up Breed's Hill and against the rebels' left flank. Murderous gunfire cut through the British ranks. The survivors retreated. Another attack was quickly organized. Again, the redcoats were repulsed with heavy **casualties**.

American soldiers on Breed's Hill near Boston await a frontal assault by the British Army. The July 1775 battle ended with the British holding the hill, but at a high cost in casualties.

After about an hour, 400 reinforcements arrived from Boston. The British mounted a third assault. This time it was directed entirely at Breed's Hill. The defenders there were running out of ammunition. British troops swarmed the redoubt and overcame the militiamen in hand-to-hand combat. The colonists fell back to Bunker Hill, then retreated across Charlestown Neck.

In the 18th century, the side that held the battlefield at the end of the fighting was considered the victor. By that standard, the British had won

THE NOBLE TRAIN OF ARTILLERY

The cannons that finally forced the British to evacuate Boston came from Fort Ticonderoga. That fort, which Patriots had captured in May 1775, was in northeastern New York. It was about 300 miles from Boston.

A young colonel named Henry Knox first approached George Washington with the idea of getting cannons from Ticonderoga. Though most of his commanders thought the idea was crazy, Washington approved the mission.

Knox arrived at Ticonderoga on December 5. He selected 59 artillery pieces. In all, they weighed an estimated 60 tons. Knox and his men moved the guns across Lake George on barges. From there, the guns were loaded onto specially built sleds pulled by teams of oxen. Men and animals struggled to get the sleds through deep snow and dense woodlands, across frozen rivers, and over the Berkshire Mountains. The "noble train of artillery," as Knox dubbed his incredible expedition, reached Cambridge in late January 1776.

This painting depicts Henry Knox's "Noble Train of Artillery," which moved 59 cannons from Fort Ticonderoga to Boston during the winter of 1775–76.

what became known as the Battle of Bunker Hill. But the cost was appalling: of about 2,400 redcoats who fought in the battle, more than 1,050 were casualties, including 226 dead. American casualties, meanwhile, totaled approximately 450, with about 115 dead. "A few more such victories," Henry Clinton recalled later, "would have shortly put an end to British dominion in America."

Extending an Olive Branch

On July 3, 1775, George Washington officially took command of the Continental Army at Cambridge, Massachusetts. In spite of the militias' recent brave performance at Bunker Hill, Washington was dismayed at the condition of the army. The troops lacked discipline. Drunkenness and brawling were common. Men routinely ignored orders from their officers. In turn, many officers seemed to have little regard for their duties. Some disappeared from camp for days or weeks on end. Clearly, Washington faced a difficult task in transforming the Continental Army into an effective fighting force.

At this point, though, most American colonists hoped to avoid a full-scale war. Patriots who favored a complete break with Great Britain were in the minority. A significant proportion of the colonial population took the Crown's side in the recent disputes. These colonists were known as Loyalists. A larger group of colonists remained neutral. They neither took up the Patriot cause nor stood with the Loyalists. Many simply wanted to go about their normal lives.

The Continental Congress made an attempt to resolve colonial disagreements with Great Britain. On July 8, the Congress sent to King George III an appeal known as the Olive Branch Petition. It expressed the American colonists' loyalty to the king. It blamed the king's ministers and Parliament for the oppressive policies that colonists disliked. And it asked the king to intercede to bring colonists relief from those policies. This, the petition suggested, would lead to "a happy and permanent reconciliation" between Great Britain and the colonies.

But King George refused to receive the Olive Branch Petition. In August, he issued a proclamation calling the Patriots traitors engaged in an open rebellion. The proclamation said that all of the king's loyal subjects were obligated to help suppress the rebellion.

King George addressed Parliament on October 26, 1775. He said more British troops and warships would be sent to America. Also, he revealed that certain foreign governments had offered their assistance. In fact, Great Britain was going to hire thousands of professional soldiers from several German states. Americans referred to these German soldiers as *Hessians*. With the additional forces, the king anticipated a speedy end to the disorder in America.

King George III believed it was appropriate for the colonies to pay part of the cost of defending them through taxes. He supported the government ministers who tried to implement plans to tax the colonies. When the Americans defied his orders, the king ordered additional British troops to America in order to re-assert royal control over the colonies.

The Siege of Boston

Meanwhile, the situation around Boston had settled into a stalemate. There was no fighting. With no way to attack the redcoats, the Continental Army simply kept them cut off in the city. The redcoats dared not risk marching out to try to break the siege.

Some fighting occurred elsewhere in the colonies, though. Patriot and *Loyalist* militias battled each other in various places in the South. Two American forces launched an invasion of Canada. One of them captured Montreal. But on December 31, 1775, the combined American forces suffered a major defeat at Quebec City.

The siege of Boston finally came to an end in March 1776. Washington's army received more than 50 artillery pieces, including large siege cannons. Most of the cannons were placed on Dorchester Heights. From that high ground south of Boston, the big guns could threaten British positions in the city as well as ships in the harbor. General Howe, who had replaced General Gage as the British commander-in-chief, decided to evacuate Boston.

One hundred twenty ships sailed out of Boston Harbor on March 17. They carried nearly 9,000 redcoats and 1,100 Loyalists to Halifax, Nova Scotia.

Independence Proclaimed

Public opinion in the colonies had been shifting. More and more people favored a complete break with Great Britain. Many colonists were influenced by a pamphlet published in January 1776. *Common Sense*, by Thomas Paine, made a strong case for independence.

Members of the committee assigned to draft the Declaration of Independence—John Adams, Roger Sherman, Robert Livingston, Thomas Jefferson, and Benjamin Franklin—present the document to John Hancock, president of the Second Continental Congress, in June 1776.

In the Continental Congress, some delegates remained wary of proclaiming American independence. But by June, momentum was clearly building toward that end. Congress assigned a five-person committee the task of preparing a document that explained the colonies' reasons for breaking away from Great Britain. Thomas Jefferson of Virginia wrote the first draft. After editing, Congress voted to approve the final version of the Declaration of Independence on July 4, 1776.

The Declaration said that all people have certain rights—such as "Life, Liberty, and the pursuit of Happiness"—that can't be forfeited or taken away. Governments are set up, with the consent of the people, to secure these rights. If a government violates the rights of the people, the people may get rid of the government and establish a new one. The Declaration proceeded to list the many ways King George III had acted to establish "an absolute Tyranny" over the colonies. And so, the colonies had dissolved their political ties with Great Britain. They were now the free and independent "united States of America."

Of course, declaring independence was one thing. Securing independence by defeating the world's most powerful military would be quite another matter.

 TEXT-DEPENDENT QUESTIONS

1. Where did the first battles of the Revolutionary War take place?

2. What was the Olive Branch Petition?

3. When, and where, was the Declaration of Independence adopted?

 RESEARCH PROJECT

Fifty-six men signed the Declaration of Independence. Pick one of them and write a short biography.

Chapter 3:

TIMES THAT TRY MEN'S SOULS

After the British withdrew from Boston, General Washington had left a small force there to hold the city. By April, he'd moved most of his army to New York City. He was determined to defend the city from an expected British attack.

(Above) Soldiers from Delaware protect the retreating Continental Army during the Battle of Long Island in August 1776. George Washington's outnumbered force was unable to prevent the British from capturing New York City in September.

Holding New York would be a tall order. The city was situated at the southern end of Manhattan Island. Washington had no warships at his disposal. The Royal Navy would be able to operate uncontested in the waters around New York.

Defeat on Long Island

Washington and his commanders oversaw the construction of defenses in New York City. They also fortified Brooklyn Heights. That high ground on Long Island lay across the East River from New York City.

As spring turned into summer, Washington's army grew. Regiments of Continental soldiers raised in several of the states arrived.

On June 29, British warships began arriving in the Lower Bay, south of New York City. In the weeks that followed, regiment upon regiment of redcoats and Hessians went ashore on Staten Island. Their numbers eventually reached about 32,000. An additional 13,000 sailors and marines manned the 400-odd ships of the British fleet.

On August 22, about 15,000 redcoat and Hessian troops were transported from Staten Island to Long Island. They landed at Gravesend Bay, more than 10 miles south of Brooklyn Heights. A few days later, another 5,000 Hessians joined them.

Washington suspected that the British move was a feint, or trick. He left more than 8,000 Continental soldiers in New York City, committing 10,000 to Long Island.

 WORDS TO UNDERSTAND IN THIS CHAPTER

bombardment—a continuous attack with bombs or cannon shells.

oath of allegiance—a statement in which a person promises to be loyal to a ruler or to his country.

WEAPONS AND TACTICS

All the firearms used in the Revolutionary War fired a single shot and were loaded from the muzzle (the front end of the barrel). Rifles were quite accurate. A skilled rifleman could reliably hit a man at a distance of 200 yards. But rifles could take a minute or more to reload. That's why most infantrymen were equipped with muskets. A well-trained soldier could fire a musket three or four times in a minute.

The effective range of a musket was about 100 yards. But consistently hitting a *specific* target beyond about 75 yards was nearly impossible. For that reason, lines of closely grouped soldiers fired together. This concentrated fire, called a volley, was bound to hit some enemy soldiers. A few volleys, fired while advancing, might break up the enemy's line enough to overwhelm it with a bayonet charge.

The bayonet was a blade of about 18 inches in length, which could be fitted into a metal sleeve on top of a musket barrel. Early in the war, many American soldiers didn't have bayonets. That put them at a distinct disadvantage.

Artillery was used on the battlefield in several ways. For example, iron cannonballs ranging from 3 to 12 pounds could be fired up to 800 yards into the ranks of approaching soldiers. A cannonball would

During the 18th century, the limited range and accuracy of muskets required armies to stand together and fire volleys at enemy forces.

kill or mangle anyone in its path. At a couple hundred yards or less, grapeshot could be used to devastating effect. Grapeshot was a packet of small iron balls that dispersed when fired.

The American plan was to stop the British along a line of hills south and east of Brooklyn Heights. But the Continentals had left a pass through the Heights of Guan undefended. Loyalists informed the British of this fact.

Ten thousand redcoats marched through the Jamaica Pass, east of the American lines, in the early morning hours of August 27. Hessian and redcoat regiments were attacking the American positions from the front when, at 9 am, the 10,000-man British force swept in from behind.

The left and center of the American line soon collapsed. Hundreds of Continental soldiers dropped their muskets and ran for their lives. Soldiers on the American right continued to fight ferociously, which allowed many of their comrades to reach the fortified positions at Brooklyn Heights. But the Battle of Brooklyn—or the Battle of Long Island, as it's also called—was over by noon. It had been a fiasco for the Continental Army. Some 300 men were dead, and another 700 or so wounded. More than 1,000, including three generals, had been captured.

Against the advice of his officers, General William Howe decided not to attack Brooklyn Heights immediately. Instead, the British commander prepared for a siege. This allowed Washington to save his army. On August 29–30, under the cover of darkness and then a dense morning fog, about 9,000 Continental troops were ferried across the East River to New York City.

New York City Lost

On September 15, British warships anchored in the East River near a place called Kips Bay unleashed a thunderous *bombardment*. When the naval guns fell silent after an hour, thousands of British and Hessian soldiers went ashore. The British planned to trap American forces to the south, in New York City.

But Washington had already decided to abandon the city. Most of the Continental Army was already north of Kips Bay. In the wake of the debacle on Long Island, Washington had come to an important realization. The American Revolution would stay alive as long as the Continental Army remained in the field. The entire army shouldn't be risked in a single engagement. Washington's aide Alexander Hamilton summed up his commander's strategy. "Our hopes are not placed in any particular city,

This French illustration from 1776 shows the city of New York in flames after the British Army captured the city in September of that year. British officers believed that Patriots had deliberately started the fire, which damaged or destroyed a large area of the city.

or spot of ground," he noted, "but in preserving a good army . . . to take advantage of favorable opportunities, and waste and defeat the enemy by piecemeal."

On September 16, a retreating American unit grew furious when British buglers played a foxhunting call. The Americans turned on their pursuers and eventually drove them back in the Battle of Harlem Heights. But that small victory was followed by a defeat at the Battle of White Plains on October 28. Three weeks later, an ill-advised decision by a young American general, Nathanael Greene, led to disaster. Greene sought to hold a fort overlooking the Hudson River. When Fort Washington was overrun on November 16, the British took more than 2,800 Americans prisoner.

Hopes Dimming

"I am wearied almost to death," a discouraged George Washington wrote to his brother. Washington began a retreat southward across New Jersey.

On December 7, the ragtag Continental Army boarded boats in Trenton and crossed the Delaware River into Pennsylvania. Washington had ordered boats on the New Jersey side of the river destroyed, to prevent the British from pursuing his army further.

By mid-December, General Howe had suspended British operations for the winter. Howe returned to New York City. He left troops in a series of outposts in New Jersey.

Most on the British side thought the war was for all intents and purposes over. "The fact is, their army is broken all to pieces," wrote Lord Rawdon, a British officer, "and the spirit of their leaders and [supporters] is all broken."

Morale in the Continental Army, and among Patriots overall, had indeed hit rock bottom. Washington's call for the New Jersey militia to turn out had gone unanswered. Thousands of New Jersey residents had sworn an **oath of allegiance** to the king in exchange for an unconditional pardon. Continental troops had deserted in droves. In addition, 2,000 had gone home on December 1, when their enlistments expired. The remainder of the Continental Army enlistments were set to expire on January 1, 1777. There seemed little reason for the men to reenlist.

The cause appeared hopeless. "These are the times that try men's souls," wrote Thomas Paine, who'd attached himself to the camp of Nathanael Greene.

On the night of December 25, 1776, the Continental Army secretly crossed the Delaware River and attacked the British garrison at Trenton. The American victory at Trenton, and another at Princeton a few days later, encouraged the colonists to keep fighting.

The Revolution Revived

Washington was determined to make one last effort to save the Revolution. On Christmas night, he led 2,400 troops across the Delaware River in the midst of a fierce winter storm. They landed about nine miles north of Trenton.

After a grueling march, Washington and his men reached Trenton around 8 am on December 26. The Americans quickly descended on the Hessian garrison occupying the town. Fighting raged for about an hour before the German professional soldiers surrendered. American casualties totaled just four wounded. Meanwhile, about 20 Hessians had been killed, and another 90 or so wounded. The Americans took 900 prisoners.

News of the victory at Trenton electrified Patriots across the nation. More important, the majority of Washington's troops reenlisted. On January 3, 1777, Washington led them to another victory, at the Battle of Princeton.

The cause of independence remained alive.

TEXT-DEPENDENT QUESTIONS

1. What were the Heights of Guan?
2. Rifles were much more accurate than muskets. So why were most troops outfitted with muskets?
3. Which battle was fought on December 26, 1776? Why was the American victory in that battle so important?

RESEARCH PROJECT

During the Revolutionary War, some women—Patriots as well as Loyalists—risked their lives to serve as spies. Check out the website of the National Women's History Museum (https://www.nwhm.org/online-exhibits/spies/2.htm). Choose one of the spies profiled there, and gather as much information about her as you can from other sources.

Chapter 4:

A TALE OF TWO CAMPAIGNS

The British launched two major campaigns in 1777. One aimed to take control of New York's Hudson River valley. The other targeted Philadelphia, the political capital and largest city in the rebellious United States.

(Above) British General John Burgoyne surrenders his sword, and his army, to Horatio Gates after the Battle of Saratoga in October 1777. The American victory at Saratoga encouraged France and other European countries to provide military supplies and troops to help the colonists.

Invasion from Canada

In June 1777, General John Burgoyne led an 8,000-man force of British regulars, Hessians, and Canadian militiamen out of Quebec. Gentleman Johnny, as Burgoyne was known, planned to move south to the Hudson River. At the same time, a smaller force would head down the St. Lawrence River to Lake Ontario, then move eastward along the Mohawk River. That force, commanded by Brigadier General Barry St. Leger, would link up with Burgoyne at Albany.

They would then drive south, down the Hudson River. General Howe, meanwhile, would lead troops north from New York City to meet them. Burgoyne thought the British would emerge from the campaign with complete control of the Hudson River valley. This would cut off the four New England colonies and, he believed, strangle the American Revolution.

At first, Burgoyne's plan went smoothly. His force moved across the length of Lake Champlain. In early July, they compelled the Americans to abandon Fort Ticonderoga.

To the west, St. Leger was also making progress. His 1,700-man force—consisting of redcoats, Canadian militia fighters, Loyalists, and Iroquois Indians—began a siege of Fort Stanwix on August 2. The fort commanded the headwaters of the Mohawk River.

An American attempt to relieve Fort Stanwix's defenders was stopped on August 6, at the uncommonly brutal Battle of Oriskany. But St. Leger's

 WORDS TO UNDERSTAND IN THIS CHAPTER

> *deplete*—to use up the resources of something.
>
> *letter of marque*—a government license that allows a private ship owner to commit actions that would otherwise be considered piracy, such as attacking and capturing enemy ships.

During the Revolutionary War, a significant number of women accompanied armies in the field. Often, they were wives of soldiers. They performed a variety of essential duties, including cooking and caring for the wounded. They shared in the hardships faced by the army and were subject to military discipline.

Indian allies were discontented in the wake of the battle. They abandoned the expedition at the approach of another American relief column. Overestimating the relief column's size, St. Leger retreated to Lake Ontario in late August. He later pulled back to Quebec.

Burgoyne, meanwhile, had run into troubles of his own. American forces chopped down large trees to block roads. They destroyed bridges. Burgoyne's column slowed to a crawl. His supplies began to run out. And Burgoyne received a letter from General Howe. It informed him that Howe would not be leading a force up the Hudson Valley, as Burgoyne expected.

By early August, the British column was still more than 50 miles north of Albany. Burgoyne detached 800 men from his main force. Commanded by Friedrich Baum, a Hessian lieutenant colonel, the detachment was to march southeast to the town of Bennington (in present-day Vermont). There, the soldiers were to seize horses, cattle, and other badly needed supplies.

A 2,000-strong American militia force quickly assembled to counter the threat. Commanded by General John Stark, it consisted largely of New Hampshire men. On August 16, Stark's force surrounded and routed Baum's

General John Stark commanded militia from New Hampshire. His men defeated part of the British army at the Battle of Bennington, Vermont.

detachment. The Americans later beat back a 600-man column sent to reinforce Baum. In all, Burgoyne lost over 900 troops at the Battle of Bennington. American casualties, meanwhile, totaled only about 70 killed and wounded.

Victory at Saratoga

Burgoyne's *depleted* force continued to move slowly southward along the Hudson River. But an American force blocked its way. The Americans fortified Bemis Heights. That high ground overlooked the Hudson south of the village of Saratoga, New York. The Americans were under the command of General Horatio Gates. An immigrant from England, Gates had previously served in the British army, where he'd risen to the rank of major. Congress had appointed him to head the Northern Department, one of the main sections of the Continental Army.

Burgoyne moved to encircle Bemis Heights. But on September 19, his army met with an American division led by General Benedict Arnold. The Battle of Freeman's Farm raged for more than three hours before the Americans finally retreated back to Bemis Heights. They'd suffered some 350 casualties. But British casualties topped 600. Many of those casualties had been inflicted by the Rifle Corps. Led by Colonel Daniel Morgan, the special unit was made up of backwoodsmen from Pennsylvania, Maryland, and Virginia. With their long rifles, they were devastating at 200 yards—twice the effective range of a musket.

After the battle, Burgoyne ordered his troops to dig in. He dispatched a letter to

General Horatio Gates (left) was an experienced officer who had served in the British army for 25 years before retiring to Virginia. As commander of the Continental Army at Saratoga, he was given credit for the victory, although the American success owed a great deal to the actions of his subordinates.

THE WAR AT SEA

In the early years of the Revolutionary War, Great Britain enjoyed naval superiority. The Royal Navy was a key instrument for supporting British land campaigns. It evacuated trapped regiments from Boston. It brought a 32,000-man invasion force to New York. It put troops in position to take Philadelphia. And the Americans were powerless to stop these movements.

The Americans used their limited naval forces mostly to disrupt British commercial shipping. The Continental Congress granted special licenses known as letters of marque to private ship captains called privateers. The letters of marque authorized privateers to attack British ships. The privateers could sell any cargo or ships they captured.

In October 1775, Congress also authorized the creation of the Continental navy. Most of its ships were purchased. They included many converted merchant vessels. Thirteen warships called frigates were ordered by Congress and built in American shipyards. But the largest of them mounted just 32 guns—no match for 70-gun British ships of the line. Of about 60 vessels that saw service in the Continental navy, fewer than a dozen survived the Revolutionary War.

John Paul Jones was the first American naval captain to defeat a British warship in battle.

The naval balance of power shifted when France—and, later, Spain and the Netherlands—joined the war against Great Britain. Their combined navies posed a serious threat to the British on the high seas.

New York City, urgently requesting help from General Henry Clinton.

By early October, the British situation had grown desperate. The troops were surviving on half rations. Their horses began dying of starvation. Burgoyne decided he needed to break out of his defensive positions.

On October 7, a large British force probed a wooded area below Bemis Heights. They were discovered, triggering the Battle of Bemis Heights. The Americans drove the British back to their defensive works. Later, rallied by Benedict Arnold, American soldiers overran a redoubt occupied by Hessians. Night brought an end to the fighting.

Burgoyne had lost another 400 men killed or wounded. He soon began a northward retreat, leaving the sick and wounded behind. But it was futile. On October 17, Gentleman Johnny surrendered his entire army near Saratoga.

Objective: Philadelphia

Three months before Burgoyne's surrender, more than 200 British ships had sailed out of Lower New York Bay. What was their target? That question preoccupied George Washington and his aides.

Washington suspected the movement was a feint, designed to get him to move the main part of the Continental Army out of northern New Jersey. That would allow General Howe to commit a large number of troops to support Burgoyne's invasion, without worrying that the Americans would take the opportunity to attack New York City.

BENEDICT ARNOLD

Benedict Arnold, a hero at Saratoga, would later become a traitor to the American cause. In 1780, he attempted to hand over to the British a strategic fort at West Point, New York. Arnold didn't think he'd received enough credit for his military accomplishments, and he was angry at being passed over for promotion. In 1780 he secretly plotted with the British to turn over the fort he commanded at West Point. The plot was uncovered, and Arnold barely escaped arrest, fleeing to England.

However, the British fleet eventually sailed up the Chesapeake Bay. On August 25, some 17,000 troops under the command of General Howe landed at Head of Elk, Maryland. They were just 45 miles southwest of Philadelphia.

Washington moved to block the British advance in southeastern Pennsylvania, at Brandywine Creek. He deployed troops on the eastern bank of the Brandywine, at every place he thought the British could cross. He expected the fighting to occur at Chad's Ford (today spelled Chadds Ford).

On the morning of September 11, several thousand Hessians and redcoats did attack around Chad's Ford. But the main body of Howe's army crossed the Brandywine about eight miles to the north, at a ford Washington didn't know about. In the afternoon, 8,000 to 10,000 British troops bore down on the American right flank.

The American right and center gave way amid fierce fighting. But a reserve division was rushed forward under General Nathanael Greene. Greene's division slowed the British advance. Washington's army was able to disengage without being destroyed. Casualties, though, had been heavy.

After the Battle of Brandywine, Washington tried to keep his forces between the British army and Philadelphia. But the British managed to maneuver around the thinly spread Continental troops. On September 26, Howe's army marched unopposed into Philadelphia. The Continental Congress had fled the city a week earlier.

Washington didn't wait long before trying to dislodge the British from Philadelphia. Early in the morning on October 4, about 11,000 American troops converged on Germantown, a

During the Battle of Germantown, near Philadelphia, British troops occupied this stone mansion and thwarted an American attack. The Continental Army was unable to prevent British troops from capturing and occupying Philadelphia, the colonies' largest city, in the fall of 1777.

few miles north of Philadelphia. But the battle plan was complicated. The attack soon went awry. After several hours of fighting, the Continental Army was compelled to withdraw.

A Crucial Alliance

The Battle of Germantown looked like another demoralizing defeat for Washington's army. But across the Atlantic Ocean 3,000 miles away, French leaders saw the battle differently. It was evidence of George Washington's courage and resolve. Washington would never give up. More important, the Continental victory at Saratoga convinced the French that the Americans could actually win the war.

On February 6, 1778, France and the United States signed the Treaty of Alliance. It committed France to joining the fight against Great Britain. Some 12,000 French soldiers would eventually be sent to America. And, critically, the French navy would challenge the Royal Navy's dominance at sea.

 TEXT-DEPENDENT QUESTIONS

1. What did the British hope to accomplish through General John Burgoyne's invasion from Canada?

2. Which battle paved the way for the British to occupy Philadelphia?

3. With which country did the United States sign a treaty on February 6, 1778?

 RESEARCH PROJECT

War brings terrible suffering to the soldiers, sailors, and other military personnel who do the fighting. But in many cases it also has profound effects on civilians. Use the library or Internet to find some firsthand accounts of what life was like for women, children, and other civilians during the Revolutionary War.

Chapter 5:
ENDURANCE AND TRIUMPH

During the winter of 1777–1778, Washington's army camped at Valley Forge, about 18 miles northwest of Philadelphia. The men suffered greatly there. They endured outbreaks of disease, chronic shortages of food, and a lack of warm clothing.

But by the time spring finally arrived, the army was a more disciplined and effective fighting force. Friedrich von Steuben deserved much of the

(Above) General Washington rides past troops at Valley Forge. Conditions at the American camp were difficult during the winter of 1777–1778, as food and warm clothing were scarce. However, as a result of intense training, George Washington's troops left camp at Valley Forge a more disciplined and effective fighting force.

WORDS TO UNDERSTAND IN THIS CHAPTER

> *backcountry*—a remote, undeveloped rural area.
>
> *federal government*—a central government intended to
> control a union of individual states.

credit for that. Von Steuben was a German volunteer with long military experience. He trained the Continentals in skills that were vital to success on the 18th-century battlefield.

Washington's soldiers soon got the chance to demonstrate their new capabilities. On June 28, 1778, the Continental Army beat back repeated British attacks at the Battle of Monmouth.

The battle was fought as a huge British column moved through New Jersey to New York. The column included the troops who'd taken Philadelphia the previous fall. With France's entry into the war, the British had decided to abandon Philadelphia.

Southern Strategy

The Battle of Monmouth would prove to be the last major engagement of the Revolutionary War fought in the northern states. The British increasingly focused their attention on the south.

The southern states had already seen their share of fighting. Patriot and Loyalist militias battled each other, often with uncommon brutality. Neighbor assaulted neighbor. Encouraged by the British, Cherokee Indians attacked settlements across Georgia and the Carolinas.

General Henry Clinton—who'd replaced William Howe as the British commander-in-chief—thought the south held the key to winning the war. His southern strategy would involve capturing key coastal cities. Meanwhile, British troops would man a string of forts in the interior of the southern states. A strong regular army presence would

The Battle of Monmouth, an American victory in June 1778, gave rise to the legend of Molly Pitcher, a woman traveling with the Continental Army who took over operation of a cannon when her husband was wounded during the battle.

buoy the spirits of the king's supporters. They'd flock to join Loyalist militias. Royal authority would gradually be reestablished.

British on the Move

In December 1778, the British took Savannah. Soon, a royal government was in place in Georgia.

South Carolina was the next target. In late 1779, General Clinton sailed from New York City with a force of about 8,500 men. He laid siege to

Charleston. When South Carolina's capital fell in May 1780, more than 5,000 American soldiers were taken prisoner.

Confident now that the southern strategy would succeed, Clinton soon returned to New York City. He left General Charles Cornwallis in charge of finishing the campaign. Cornwallis was to consolidate control over South Carolina, then take North Carolina. After that, he would march into Virginia. British control of Virginia, the most populous state, might spell the end of the Revolution.

Ignoring the wishes of George Washington, Congress appointed General Horatio Gates to command the Continental Army's Southern Department.

American and French soldiers attack the British fortifications at Savannah, Georgia, in October 1779. However, the siege of Savannah failed to drive out the British, and by August 1780 the British held a strong position in the southern colonies.

AFRICAN AMERICANS IN THE REVOLUTIONARY WAR

"We hold these truths to be self-evident," the Declaration of Independence famously said, "that all men are created equal." At the time, though, there were half a million black slaves in America—and the Continental Congress had no plans to free them.

Still, an estimated 5,000 African Americans served in the Continental Army during the eight years of the Revolutionary War. Several hundred more served in the Continental navy.

Some black soldiers were freemen. But many were slaves promised their freedom in exchange for military service. Most African Americans in the Continental Army came from the northern states. Maryland was the only southern state that permitted the enlistment of blacks.

For their part, the British promised freedom to all runaway slaves. Tens of thousands, mostly in the south, took them up on that promise. But only a few thousand African Americans were ever incorporated into the ranks of British military units. Far more served as laborers.

Gates—who'd received much more credit for the victory at Saratoga than he actually deserved—soon blundered into a disaster.

Gates moved against Camden, a British supply hub in the interior of South Carolina. On the morning of August 16, 1780, he faced off against Lord Cornwallis. The American force enjoyed a significant advantage in troop numbers—about 3,100 versus 2,200. But Gates deployed inexperienced militia on his left flank, opposite the best regiments Cornwallis had. The redcoats fired a volley and immediately charged. The militiamen, who had no bayonets, ran away in panic. Continentals from Delaware and Maryland fought valiantly on the American right. Once British infantry and cavalry had gotten behind them, though, nothing could prevent a rout.

In just an hour of fighting, the Americans suffered more than 900 dead and wounded. Another thousand were captured. The remnants of Gates's army were scattered.

The Tide Begins to Turn

With his huge victory at the Battle of Camden, Cornwallis thought he'd secured South Carolina. He moved his army into North Carolina, occupying Charlotte. To the west, a large Loyalist militia force moved in tandem with Cornwallis's army. But on October 7, American militiamen smashed the Loyalists at the Battle of Kings Mountain. Cornwallis put his plans to take North Carolina on hold. He pulled back to Winnsboro, South Carolina.

After the disaster at Camden, the Continental Congress decided that George Washington should select Horatio Gates's replacement. Washington chose Nathanael Greene.

In early December, Greene arrived in Charlotte to take command of the southern army. He was shocked by what he found. "Nothing can be more wretched and distressing than the condition of the troops," he wrote to Washington, "starving with cold and hunger, without tents and camp equipage. Those of the Virginia line are literally naked, and a great part totally unfit for any kind of duty."

But within a couple weeks, Greene got his shell of an army into action. He divided his force in two, and both groups moved across the border into South Carolina. Daniel Morgan, now a brigadier general,

General Nathanael Greene, one of Washington's most trusted subordinates, was sent to reorganize the American army in the South after the disastrous defeat at the Battle of Camden in August 1780.

American cavalry, wearing green, battle with the British cavalry commanded by Colonel Banastre Tarleton at the Battle of Cowpens in January 1780. The victory at Cowpens encouraged Patriots in the South to keep fighting while weakening the British army. Daniel Morgan's small army captured more than 700 British soldiers and killed 110, with only 12 Americans killed and 60 wounded.

took 600 men to the western part of the state. Greene, with the remaining 1,600 or so, threatened the east.

To stop Morgan, Cornwallis dispatched a 1,150-man force under the command of Colonel Banastre Tarleton. Among Patriots, Tarleton had a reputation for ruthlessness. "Bloody Ban," it was said, had massacred militiamen after they'd surrendered at a May 1780 battle. But Tarleton proved no match for Daniel Morgan, whose force had been bolstered by the arrival of hundreds of militia. On January 17, 1781, Morgan's men crushed the redcoats at the Battle of Cowpens. British losses totaled about 900. American casualties, meanwhile, were only a dozen dead and 60 wounded.

An Army Exhausted

Morgan's detachment soon reunited with the rest of the army. Cornwallis set out after the Americans. To speed up the pursuit, he ditched his supply wagons. But Greene managed to stay one step ahead. He led the 2,500 redcoats on an exhausting chase north through the rugged *backcountry* of North Carolina. Finally, on February 14, the American army crossed the Dan River into Virginia. Lacking boats, Cornwallis couldn't pursue any further.

But after a week resting and refitting his troops, Greene crossed back into North Carolina. He prepared for battle at Guilford Courthouse. He now had about 4,400 men, though many were untested militia.

The British arrived at Guilford Courthouse on March 15. The grueling pursuit of Greene had depleted their ranks to about 2,100. The redcoats were almost 250 miles from their closest supply base. They'd had to resort to eating some of their horses to stave off hunger. Many of the men were sick.

None of that seemed to dampen the redcoats' ferocity. The Battle of Guilford Courthouse was a brutal struggle that raged for two and a half hours. At one point, the Americans appeared to be overwhelming a section of the British line in savage hand-to-hand combat. Cornwallis ordered his artillery to fire directly into the line, killing Continentals and redcoats alike.

Greene at last withdrew, allowing Cornwallis to claim victory. But British

During the Revolutionary War, far more soldiers died from disease than were killed in battle.

casualties exceeded 500, or about a quarter of Cornwallis's force. The army would never fully recover.

Victory at Yorktown

Cornwallis gave up on controlling the Carolinas. He moved his army into Virginia and took command of other British forces operating there.

Cornwallis eventually established a base of operations at Yorktown. Its location, on the York River near the Chesapeake Bay, would enable the army to be resupplied or evacuated by ship.

In August 1781, George Washington received word that a French fleet was headed for Virginia. Washington and the French general Jean-Baptiste de Rochambeau saw a chance to trap Cornwallis at Yorktown.

On August 19, some 4,000 French and 3,000 Continental soldiers set off from Dobbs Ferry, New York. They arrived in the vicinity of Yorktown in late September. Joining thousands of American and French troops already there, they surrounded Yorktown.

On September 5, a French fleet had defeated a British fleet near the mouth of the Chesapeake. With the bay under the control of the French navy, Cornwallis's army couldn't be reinforced or evacuated.

In early October, French and American soldiers dug a trench around the perimeter of the redcoats' lines. They built emplacements for the artillery. On October 9, siege guns roared to life. The big guns pounded the British positions relentlessly.

On the night of October 14, American and French troops stormed two redoubts that formed the last significant part of the British outer defenses. Cornwallis surrendered five days later. More than 7,000 redcoats and Hessians were taken prisoner. Yorktown would be the last major battle of the war.

Independence Secured

When news of Cornwallis's surrender reached London, support for the war in Parliament eroded. By the spring of 1782, the British had opened peace negotiations with the United States.

On September 3, 1783, American and British representatives signed the Treaty of Paris. It officially ended the Revolutionary War. Great Britain gave up all claims to the 13 colonies. It recognized them as "free, sovereign, and independent states."

When Lord Cornwallis surrendered his British army at Yorktown, Virginia, in October 1781, it marked the end of major combat in the American Revolution. The war officially ended when British and American officials signed a peace treaty in Paris on September 3, 1783.

During the Revolution, the American colonies were united under a framework of government called the Articles of Confederation. This agreement enabled the 13 colonies to work together. After the war ended, however, it was clear that a stronger **federal government** was needed. In 1787, a new framework of government, the U.S. Constitution, was drafted and ratified by the states. For more than 225 years, the Constitution has been the basis for government in the United States.

For the United States, independence had been won at considerable cost. Precise casualty figures will never be known. But many historians believe that about 25,000 Americans lost their lives in the Revolutionary War. If correct, this would mean that the war claimed nearly 1 of every 100 people living in the 13 states at the time.

How, and why, had Patriots endured such sacrifice? "Remember officers and soldiers," George Washington had once urged his troops, "that you are free men, fighting for the blessings of liberty." That simple idea had proved irresistible.

TEXT-DEPENDENT QUESTIONS

1. Who took command of the Continental Army's Southern Department after the disastrous Battle of Camden?

2. Why was the Battle of the Capes important?

3. Where was the final major battle of the Revolutionary War?

RESEARCH PROJECT

The Revolutionary War officially ended in 1783. But some historians say the American Revolution wasn't complete until 1789. That year, a new federal government began under the United States Constitution. Read about the Constitution. How, and why, was it drafted? How was it ratified? Incorporate what you learn into a timeline.

CHRONOLOGY

1763   The Seven Years' War ends. A proclamation by King George III bars British North American colonists from settling west of the Appalachian Mountains.

1765   Parliament passes the Stamp Act, but colonial opposition prevents it from going into effect.

1766   Parliament repeals the Stamp Act but passes the Declaratory Act.

1767   The Townshend Acts are passed.

1768   British troops are sent to Boston.

1770   All the Townshend duties are repealed, except the one on tea. The Boston Massacre takes place on March 5.

1773   Parliament passes the Tea Act. In December, Patriots dump more than 340 chests of tea into Boston Harbor, an event remembered as the Boston Tea Party.

1774   Parliament passes the Coercive Acts. The First Continental Congress meets in Philadelphia from September to October.

1775   War begins on April 19 with fighting at Lexington and Concord and along the road to Boston. The Second Continental Congress convenes in Philadelphia, voting in June to create the Continental Army. On June 17, the British suffer more than 1,000 casualties at the Battle of Bunker Hill. In December, Patriots are defeated at the Battle of Quebec.

1776   The British evacuate Boston in March. On July 4, Congress votes to approve the Declaration of Independence. In September, the British occupy New York City. On December 26, the Continental Army wins the Battle of Trenton.

1777   British general John Burgoyne leads an invasion from Canada. His army fails to reach Albany, New York, and Burgoyne ultimately surrenders near Saratoga, New York. In September, a British Army under General William Howe captures Philadelphia.

1778   In February, France and the United States sign the Treaty of Alliance. The British abandon Philadelphia in June and withdraw to New York City. The British and Continental armies clash at the Battle of Monmouth, New Jersey, on June 28. In December, British forces capture Savannah, Georgia.

1780   In fighting in South Carolina, the British win major victories by capturing Charleston (May 12) and routing the American southern army at the Battle of Camden (Aug. 16). Patriot militiamen smash Loyalists at the Battle of Kings Mountain (Oct. 7).

1781   The Battle of Cowpens on January 17), in northern South Carolina, is a huge American victory. After an exhausting pursuit across North Carolina, a British army under Lord Cornwallis engages the American army at the Battle of Guilford Courthouse on March 15. The British claim victory, but suffer a casualty rate of 25 percent. In September, the Battle of the Capes prevents the British from reinforcing or evacuating Cornwallis's army at Yorktown, Virginia. American and French forces begin a siege of Yorktown. On October 19, Cornwallis surrenders his army of more than 7,000 men.

1783   The Treaty of Paris is signed on September 3, officially ending the Revolutionary War. The British acknowledge the independence of the United States.

CHAPTER NOTES

p. 13: "The first Man . . ." Edwin G. Burrows and Mike Wallace, *Gotham: A History of New York City to 1898* (New York: Oxford University Press, 1998), p. 199.

p. 15: "full power and authority . . ." Edmund Sears Morgan, ed., *Prologue to Revolution: Sources and Documents on the Stamp Act Crisis, 1764–1766* (Chapel Hill: University of North Carolina Press, 1959), p. 155.

p. 20: "The die is now cast . . ." Don Cook, *The Long Fuse: How England Lost the American Colonies, 1760–1785* (New York: Atlantic Monthly Press, 1995), p. 197.

p. 24: "exert every power . . ." Frank E. Grizzard, *George Washington: A Biographical Companion* (Santa Barbara, CA: ABC-CLIO, 2002), p. 378.

p. 27: "A few more such victories . . ." Andrew Jackson O'Shaughnessy, *The Men Who Lost America: British Leadership, the American Revolution, and the Fate of the Empire* (New Haven, CT: Yale University Press, 2013), p. 86.

p. 27: "a happy and permanent . . ." Journals of the Continental Congress—Petition to the King; July 8, 1775. *The Avalon Project: Documents in Law, History and Diplomacy.* http://avalon.law.yale.edu/18th_century/contgong_07-08-75.asp

p. 30: "Life, Liberty . . ." Declaration of Independence. http://www.archives.gov/exhibits/charters/declaration_transcript.html

p. 30: "an absolute Tyranny," Ibid.

p. 34: "Our hopes are not placed . . ." John E. Ferling, *The First of Men: A Life of George Washington* (New York: Oxford University Press, 2010), p. 132.

p. 35: "I am wearied . . ." David McCullough, *1776* (New York: Simon & Schuster, 2005), p. 244.

p. 36: "The fact is . . ." Ibid., p. 251.

p. 36: "These are the times . . ." David Freeman Hawke, *Paine* (New York: Harper & Row, 1974), p. 59.

p. 50: "We hold these truths . . ." Declaration of Independence. http://www.archives.gov/exhibits/charters/declaration_transcript.html

p. 51: "Nothing can be more wretched . . ." Terry Golway, *Washington's General: Nathanael Greene and the Triumph of the American Revolution* (New York: Henry Holt, 2006), p. 239.

p. 55: "free, sovereign . . ." The Definitive Treaty of Peace 1783. *The Avalon Project: Documents in Law, History and Diplomacy.* http://avalon.law.yale.edu/18th_century/paris.asp

p. 57: "Remember officers and soldiers . . ." McCullough, *1776*, p. 159.

FURTHER READING

Catel, Patrick. *Battles of the Revolutionary War* (Why We Fought). Portsmouth, NH: Heinemann, 2010.

De Pauw, Linda Grant. *Founding Mothers: Women of America in the Revolutionary Era*. Boston: Houghton Mifflin Harcourt, 1994.

Ferling, John. *Almost a Miracle: The American Victory in the War of Independence*. New York: Oxford University Press, 2007.

McCullough, David. *1776*. New York: Simon & Schuster, 2005.

Middlekauff, Robert. *The Glorious Cause: The American Revolution, 1763–1789*. New York: Oxford University Press, 2007.

Strum, Richard M. *Causes of the American Revolution* (The Road to War: Causes of Conflict). Stockton, NJ: OTTN Publishing, 2005.

Troiani, Don, and James L. Kochan. *Don Troiani's Soldiers of the American Revolution*. Mechanicsburg, PA: Stackpole Books, 2007.

INTERNET RESOURCES

http://www.pbs.org/ktca/liberty/

The companion website to the PBS series *Liberty! The American Revolution.*

http://www.loc.gov/teachers/classroommaterials/ presentationsandactivities/presentations/timeline/amrev/ amrev.html

This guide to the American Revolution includes materials adapted for use in the classroom. It's maintained by the Library of Congress.

http://www.westpoint.edu/history/sitepages/american%20revolution.aspx

This site, from the History Department of the United States Military Academy, offers excellent maps of the Revolutionary War's major campaigns and battles.

http://memory.loc.gov/ammem/gwhtml/gwhome.html

Search George Washington's papers, including his Revolutionary War correspondence, at this site maintained by the Library of Congress.

Publisher's Note: The websites listed on this page were active at the time of publication. The publisher is not responsible for websites that have changed their address or discontinued operation since the date of publication. The publisher reviews and updates the websites each time the book is reprinted.

INDEX

Numbers in ***bold italics*** refer to captions.

SERIES GLOSSARY

blockade—an effort to cut off supplies, war material, or communications by a particular area, by force or the threat of force.

guerrilla warfare—a type of warfare in which a small group of combatants, such as armed civilians, use hit-and-run tactics to fight a larger and less mobile traditional army. The purpose is to weaken an enemy's strength through small skirmishes, rather than fighting pitched battles where the guerrillas would be at a disadvantage.

intelligence—the analysis of information collected from various sources in order to provide guidance and direction to military commanders.

logistics—the planning and execution of movements by military forces, and the supply of those forces.

salient—a pocket or bulge in a fortified line or battle line that projects into enemy territory.

siege—a military blockade of a city or fortress, with the intent of conquering it at a later stage.

tactics—the science and art of organizing a military force, and the techniques for using military units and their weapons to defeat an enemy in battle.